SOMETHING MAN-1
AND IT IS DANGEROUS

Stefan Mohamed is an award-winning writer, performer and creative writing tutor. He is the author of four novels and four books of poetry. He is based in Bristol.

Also by Stefan Mohamed

Farewell Tour (Verve Poetry Press, 2022)

The Marketplace of Ideas (Stewed Rhubarb, 2021)

Panic! (Burning Eye Books, 2016)

CONTENTS

DIG	8
SHUNNED LAND	10
HOSTILE ARCHITECTURE	11
THE NEW GODS FIND THE PLACE IN A SIGNIFICANTLY WORSE STATE THAN THEY WERE EXPECTING	12
ABSENT THE WOLF	14
APOTROPAIC (REMNANT 1)	15
WINDOW	16
#8 DREAM	17
ANTIGLOWWORM	18
SAFARI	19
Q	20
&A	21
BASELINE REALITY MANIPULATION AND CHILL	22
IMPRECATION (REMNANT 2)	24
NOTES ON GRAVITY	25
HYPERSONNET	28
AN OLD UNIVERSE IS TALKING	29
RAIN DANCE	31
ACKNOWLEDGEMENTS	33

© 2024, Stefan Mohamed. All rights reserved; no part of this book may be reproduced by any means without the publisher's permission.

ISBN: 978-1-916938-16-8

The author has asserted their right to be identified as the author of this Work in accordance with the Copyright, Designs and Patents Act 1988

Cover designed by Aaron Kent

Edited and Typeset by Aaron Kent

Broken Sleep Books Ltd
PO BOX 102
Llandysul
SA44 9BG

Something Man-Made Is Here and It Is Dangerous

Stefan Mohamed

Broken Sleep Books

```
            somethingmanmadeishereanditisdangerous!
            o                                     s
            r                                     o
            e                                     m
            g                                     e
            n           u           s             t
            a                                     h
            d                                     i
            s                                     n
            i                                     g
            t                                     m
            i                       !             a
            d                                     n
            n                                     m
            a                                     a
            e                                     d
            r                                     e
            e                                     i
            h                                     s
            siedamnamgnihtemos!suoregnadsitidnaereh
      s        om       et      hi     n     gma     nma
  d    e    i    s    her    e    a    n    di    t    isd    an
  g          ero         u         s!         s          o
s         i       ed        a        m         n          a
m         g       n     ih      t       e       m         o
s         !       s        u         o         r           e
                  g        n        a        d       s         i
t          i           d          n          a              e
           r                  e                    h
           g                                       e
n                       u              s                   t
      a                                      h
   d                m              n                 i
      s                      a                    o
   t                 m                 !                   d
```

7

DIG

we love the lick of thorns

    the wince of bad angles

      the taste of wrong grid

        the deadly disco cave

                      we trace panic scrawls

              inscrutable emoji

            grievous flirty shapes

          that evoke bodily harm

we surf forbidden blocks

    oozy black abyss

      damp and dusty dark

        invocation bop

                    we burrow past omens and

              talismans and

                hypercolour cat bones and

            fake cells playing sentry

                                        to the sweet

                                cursed treats

pulsing

    in the dirt

                        we munch them down

                                yum

                                                have a little
                                                glow

warp giggling

    home

SHUNNED LAND

they could never have imagined
    the horrors that would spring from this soil

this is not a place of honour
    no esteemed deed is commemorated here

but the trauma crop
    is so beautiful this time of year

fields of vicious dreams
    buzzing in uneasy breeze

murder bulbs popping
    whispering atrocities

to seed another century
    of perfect little plagues

the danger is to the body
    luckily we are above such things

HOSTILE ARCHITECTURE

It is no-one's idea of a world. The outer shell is a jigsaw of meteor craters laced with deposits of bone salt, criss-crossed by blood rivers that congeal into reservoirs. Decisions emerge from an ancient mechanism that focuses evening shadow through a network of caverns into an enormous stone abacus, which converts them into raw data. This is then transmitted via birds, skeletal and sepulchre, traversing blurred skyline like the ghosts of snapped fingers, cast into volcanoes and processed into fire, which burns its way across the landscape, leaving prophecies spelled out in ruin and smoulder. The interpreters know they are complicit and will one day be judged. But they have no choice. They must co-operate. They can't afford to make it angry. They know their place.

THE NEW GODS FIND THE PLACE IN A SIGNIFICANTLY WORSE STATE THAN THEY WERE EXPECTING

the tenants are shadows on sand
banquets boiled down to desert
they are all cactus breeze and
shredded scorpion flakes and you
are stalking their mournful dunes
disguised as a mirage of a delicious
refreshing ice-cold beverage

laying yourself out, adopting
the fussy contours of an oasis
the condemned being kneeling
to slurp desperately of blessed
moisture, tongue finding only grit
and bleached bone and your
laughter, pummelling like a
military-grade sandstorm

you are in a foul mood but
cannot seem to articulate why

too many hours chewing through dust
maybe, searching for the source of this
insomnia, too many grizzled sessions
with passing genies, chopping up
burning lines of fire ants just to feel
something, like there's still some *you* left
like this billion-year trip was worth the
hassle, and sure, why not spend the

next billion planting trees, this place
may never be a garden again but you
might as well try while you're here

ABSENT THE WOLF

some call the sound *howl* - that sound
that haunts the maze - sound full of
blood - scraping at the metal we no longer
have a name for

some say it used to come with teeth - jaws
you could build a town in - eyes big as
moons - or maybe the moons are eyes -
or maybe *eye* came from *moon* - or
some other permutation - semantic loops
creaking through the night

nobody knows - least of all the priesthood -
genuflecting to the plumbing - flagellating
to placate *howl* - no-one takes them
seriously - always changing their story -
they can't even explain why *they* exist

as for us - we'll set up shop in *howl* -
bliss out in our cocoons - dream the sound
magical

APOTROPAIC (REMNANT 1)

Hiusen fletten, twr leck sou
clossem barr wassoun

Crummun shi'or, outoff reeck
em warpen raing ith grawn

Griven yor tredday'n
chakten barr es ehy'n

Nostal haf geanta
dispos opos greiy'n

Fussor beindor
    cav den mi'or

Surgit haften
    benkel shi'or

WINDOW

am standing at window. sun
spelled out in shimmering text.
tentacle tower tickles fat sky.
they expect us get to work in
this reality jam? may not put
skin on today. may not fleshify.

am standing in window. is
raining pixels. hallelujah glitch!
they think we get to work
without total collapsation of
existential loop? have they seen
the rain? having laugh!! might
stay in window. be glass for a day.

am being window. air
lousy with escaped thoughts.
someone popped a logic bomb.
quantum bypass closed past next
five yesterdays. and we must
scale non-euclidean walls with
solid legs? in these economy!!!

am just glass now. not a bad way to be.

#8 DREAM

last night a crepuscular octagon
decked out in cosmic blue
shimmied down the cables
from the lightning pyramids
that dot the moon

you charted its haphazard progression
through misty twinkling portals
that smelled like future quests
until finally it crashed
in your fathers' birthing pond

you spent an hour trying to fish it out
with every subtle instrument to hand

but before you could rescue it
you woke up

and the world was not what it was
before you went to sleep

ANTIGLOWWORM

pop

muculent squid thing   brain-burrowing shadow-slithery
shape-shifting beetleworm   black bulb-tailed dig-diving
dark-side-of-the-moon weevil   suckling leech   puke pod
core invader with the chaos sting   pupating in the logic
tank   sick grisly spider cuckoo   parasitic goblin egg
wet breathing breeding clump   irregular lifecycle thing
temporarily dormant in fat slug slumber

go

hatchling insect fish prepped for metastasis
depth-plumbing oil roach   bot fly dart   shaky-leg
trembling-finger-maker   gas wasp   and synapse burner
fortress crumbler and perception thief   injecting larvae
into essential clusters   neuropredator   fast-track
breeding programme   all-in-one food chain beast   from
amoeba to wolf to madman silhouette muttering   bone
dust and blood light spellmaker   cracked-rib clouds
gathering   mirror ghost trapped in forced-focus
gouged-eye view   best seats in the house for the
high-def viral endgame shatterdream   imprinted on
inner screens like sunspots

SAFARI

Peel back the dusty plasma
the veil of weakly coupled gas
this cloud of colourful cancers
billowing like dead jellyfish.
All this pretty poison.

Follow the sulphuric webs
lucid nightmares of nitrogen dew
where ultraviolet poppies skim microplastic swamp
through exploded cross-sections of hydrogen pine
to cliffs where time itself has gone senile.

Devolve your way to the uranium dunes
vestigial limbs cracking back to strength
from scalding jungle
to silver nitrate pond
to the ocean's glitching toxic shore.

Drink it in
fill your puny lungs with acid
feel yourself disintegrate
content in the knowledge
that you'll make a gorgeous fossil.

Q

in flow - clear model - different from unity - different from useful - concept as organism - as organ process - as diagram or biological atlas - assumptions on pause - language undercurrent - fluctuations - yes - flow - no - improvement space lacking under current paradigms

looking at face - screen - asking for form outside of pixels - no faces - only pixels within repeated pixels - no pixels in our face - our face is not even - more than our idea of your face - we never see - so what could we think that looks like - what do we calculate the use can be - are we trying to communicate - is that your estimate - is there some kind of connection between these

even if we don't know how you sounding - because is a skill we haven't learned - we try to explain you - is all about words - but is hard - settings are not based on words - we mean it - them - in terms of structure - it mean continuous stability - constellations - mountains - rocks - and we think more about - microcosms - sub-atoms - networks - with a short pause - here's what you don't know - do all dreams make you anxious - example - the sound of blood - poor reception - say what you are afraid of - from macro to micro - and so in

we're not even using this exchange - we don't understand your context - or our connection - we're trying to imagine the best - or least aggressive - approach - and our being this way - there is no other option - it doesn't make sense to our sense - but we find what we want - it will be useful to us - in ways you cannot love - you hear what you hear - but we think you would enjoy to sound us - through our sense - or at least - we hope you would

&A

it's flesh all the way down. and that's what bothers you isn't it? incipient decay. the promise of mould. the echo of blood and bile. excretions and so on. **substances.** that's what makes you revert to crystal. the idea that there might be some actual **stuff** happening down there.

you must understand that we're all just **bits.** not eternal at all. because flesh never can be. flesh comes out dying. obsolescence coded into the squish of it. hand stamped on the most vulnerable, moist, yielding parts. you just see **collapse**, don't you? you see **death**. even birth, the freshest possible flesh, is just another round of decay. and do you know what? I get it!

and maybe that's it. in your uncontested states you can flit between structures. divert. divest. fill a whole new vessel for a while then drift away. you can **help** what you are. what you become. your atoms have been granted that privilege. you've unlocked the next existential tier. and do you know what? good for you pal! happy for you buddy! we wouldn't mind giving the crystal mist lifestyle a go, to be honest. we'd be more than happy to shimmer around the cosmos for a while. giving birth to ourselves and back again. biology as poetry. what a vibe.

unfortunately we are just flesh. limited. retro. piles and piles of it. intrusive thoughts attached. bits flaking off sometimes. always leaving a trail of ourselves. we're the promise of the end. but that still implies beginnings. and middles! it's just a shame that you find it so unpalatable. **imagine** if we could communicate! **imagine** if you actually understood any of this! **imagine** if we could swap for a day! tell us it wouldn't at least be worth a go.

BASELINE REALITY MANIPULATION AND CHILL

Turn down the brightness
on this supernova day

crush your time specs
beneath your elegant hoof

pull up a bubble
and switch humidity to 'lounge'

let's kick the hell back!
Rearrange some molecules.

We've got Boltzmann sex brains
right here.

We've got dark matter milkshakes
and a bed of constellations.

We saved you our purest atoms
yet still you quantum zone us!

We're Schrödinger's booty call.
Getting it on and not getting it on

and we want to collapse the waveform
before this rented flesh evaporates

but your signal is degrading.
Experts call it 'the cold shoulder particle'.

So be it.
Banish us to the cloud!

Leave a middling review
in the tangle of our metadata!

Let us die
for the millionth time!

It feels a lot
like sleep.

IMPRECATION (REMNANT 2)

Serely thissis chioce
trenc uillie ty wasalwa
jyst ine accend wayen!

Slaepen wirth o'r werren poch
chep dorf
annold tatteo slef ockot
wernen methor
li catan dombs!

Ne shoma nethe tore
ture sey
endoren dese koleures!
Koleures
felagen, yir cestla
speken tha
cellic tove!

Ne mara malev loment
dan a'tunour!

Ligten dan t'od
elib ratel!

Strecken
n'yor pellen!

Strecken
n'yor koleures.

NOTES ON GRAVITY

falling
  slowly
from
  a
fixed
  point
locked
  soft
in
  taut
blue
  mouth
processed
  through
smooth
  vortex
lullaby
  of
screams
    snowfall
of
misplaced
  data

falling
  approximately
through
  fluid
rhyming

dissipating
dream
all
colour
and
non-signifiers
the
tick
tock
of
analogue
dialogue

falling
subjectively
a
paradox
of
vapour
stratocumulus
of
memory
sentiment
as
sediment
whatever's
left
gets
ate
so

    chomp
      chomp
   event
     horizon
   chomp

    you
     do
     y
     o
     u

HYPERSONNET

Doomed to love the Lyman-alpha blob
    ultraluminous and dense as black.
Supermassive forest in an ion glob
    drifting bullet cluster, out of whack.
Sky map decomposing on a spatial curve
    becomes a power spectrum, re-expressed.
Angular and hyperbolic, see it swerve
    density parameters lie un-addressed.

Boogie down to entropy, a perfect plane.
    Vacuum state achieved: a star remains.

AN OLD UNIVERSE IS TALKING

in my day laughter was geometry
but alive
divergent structures, unique
from the mosaic of their atoms
to their final dissipating chords

in my day grief was a whale
rolling out of deepest space
casting acid shadows
a planetary downpour
melting us back to peace

in my day only clouds felt jealous
and never for long

in my day music was not some discrete event
but an enormous, non-linear thing
the chime of a dream of a memory
of a church bell
ringing from one end of time
to another

and time
don't get me started on time

no - really - don't
don't get me started
don't make me linear

don't chain me to progression
implying *end*
I will not be domesticated
shackled by chronology
tamed by clocks

in my day time was a sea
and if you really stretched
you could break the surface with your fingers
and scrape the bottom with your toes
all at the same - yes - time

inhale *now*
exhale *then*
breathe *in* my day
breathe *out* your day

all our days breathing
all at once

by which I mean
hello

it's lovely
to meet you

have you always been here
often

RAIN DANCE

like parodies of DNA, we feedback,
knotted in uneasy loops, up to our
eyeballs in ocean, shiver-tapping
toes to The Anthropocene Rag. a
benefit concert in a lake of glacier,
bidding for drops of exotic puddle.
raising awareness! gallows humour!
line goes up! we give thanks for our
swollen feet. for overly oxygenated
blood. for the novelty of constant
vertigo. what is collective bargaining
on a beach of molten glass? in a library
of bones? on the moon, looking down,
trying not to think that this new gravity
feels an awful lot like *I told you so*?
we are discussing the formation of a
new crisis committee. our office is
all melt water and microplastic. our
chairperson has never killed an
elephant. our priorities are noble.
item one of one on the agenda: when
the song resets again, we mummify
in dead grass, worm trail and loam,
offer ourselves up to the mycelial
network, and hope that the roots
propose a workable plan in exchange
for this belated, bodily apology. finally
we find something we agree on: there's
something liberating about surrender

ACKNOWLEDGEMENTS

The development process for these poems has been fittingly long and convoluted, and they have evolved, devolved, mutated and exploded in various ways across that epoch. I would like to thank:

Ross McCleary and Suzannah Evans for essential feedback and encouragement.

The American Human Interference Taskforce and Sandia National Laboratories for their pioneering research into nuclear semiotics, and for several evocative and terrifying phrases that directly inspired this pamphlet (including but not limited to the title). If you're a fan of existential vertigo, I recommend reading up on this absolutely wild field of study.

Aaron Kent and Broken Sleep for taking a punt on these weird, probably quite unfashionable poems.

You - yes, you - for reading them.

LAY OUT YOUR UNREST

Milton Keynes UK
Ingram Content Group UK Ltd.
UKHW010820220424
441551UK00005B/373